GLADIATOR
FACT FILE

MIKE CORBISHLEY

THE BRITISH MUSEUM PRESS

HOW DID I END UP AS A GLADIATOR?

"How did I end up as a gladiator?"…was a question many people must have asked themselves in the time of the Roman empire. Most gladiators were forced to fight for their lives but a few actually volunteered for the 'games', as the Romans called this deadly entertainment.

CAPTIVES, SLAVES AND CRIMINALS

Very large numbers of men, and a few women, were needed as gladiators. The main supply came from those captured in war or taken in slavery. A much smaller number of gladiators were criminals condemned to be executed. Some were given the chance to fight and they could, if they fought well and stayed alive for three years, be given their freedom.

The tombstone of a retiarius (see page 6) who died in the 3rd century AD. He has his weapons and armour, but not his net.

A mosaic from North Africa showing different types of gladiators.

FIGHTING FACTS

Although some gladiators were reported to have survived forty or fifty fights, your chance of survival was much more like 9:1 and you could expect to last no more than three years. A gladiator named Urbicius, whose gravestone has been found, had the luck and skill to survive thirteen fights in the amphitheatres. (You can read some advice and hints from Urbicius in The Gladiator's Guide to Survival).

VOLUNTEER TO BE A GLADIATOR?

A few chose to be gladiators. They volunteered to fight for their pay for a certain amount of time. Some young men from good Roman families fought as gladiators to show off. Their fights were usually 'fixed'. The fights which the emperor Nero entered were certainly fixed but a more serious gladiator was the emperor Commodus. He trained as a secutor (see page 6) and often fought hand-to-hand in the afternoon games after taking part in the wild animal hunts (see page 10) in the morning.

This vase was found in Colchester, England, and shows a retiarius called Valentinus (right) holding up a finger as a sign to beg for mercy - he has dropped his trident. The winner, on the left, is a secutor called Memnon.

ACTION TIME

TRY TO WIN YOUR WAY TO FREEDOM AS A GLADIATOR IN THE WINNERS AND LOSERS BOARD GAME.

BASIC TRAINING

Providing entertainment for the public in Roman amphitheatres was an expensive business. Politicians who paid for the gladiatorial games (called *editores*) relied on agents (*lanistae*) to train and supply the fighters.

ACTION TIME

PUT UP THE POSTER ON YOUR WALL TO REMIND YOU OF THE TRAINING YOU'LL NEED TO DO TO BECOME A GLADIATOR.

THE GLADIATORS IN THE TRAINING SCHOOLS PROBABLY WANTED TO CONTACT THEIR FAMILIES AND FRIENDS – WE DON'T KNOW IF THEY WERE ALLOWED TO WRITE HOME. YOU COULD USE THE POSTCARDS AND THE ROMAN WRITING TABLETS IN THE KIT TO SEND YOUR OWN MESSAGES.

TRAINING SCHOOLS

Schools for gladiators were known as *ludi* and were established in various parts of the Roman world. There were four schools, holding a total of about 2,000 gladiators, next to the Colosseum (see page 14) in the capital city, Rome. But the most important school in Italy itself was at Capua. Julius Caesar kept 5,000 gladiators in the gladiators' school there. The *lanistae* had a bad reputation for treating their men cruelly – we know that some gladiators in Pompeii were kept chained up in cramped conditions.

"A wooden stake was planted in the ground by each recruit, in such a way that it stuck up about 6 feet and could not sway. Against this stake the recruit practised with his wickerwork shield and wooden stave as if he were fighting a real enemy."
Vegetius (a Roman writer) in AD 80

RAW RECRUITS

When the recruits were brought to their training school, usually at the age of seventeen or eighteen, they chose a 'stage' name and their trainer set about preparing them for their first match. Each recruit was trained for six months as a particular type of gladiator, depending on his ability and build. Training was hard and before he fought other men he had to develop his skills and his muscles.

ALL SORTS OF GLADIATORS

Gladiators fought each other for entertainment so the different sorts of fighters, who fought in pairs, made the show more exciting.

RETIARIUS

The gladiator known as a retiarius fought with a net and a three-pronged spear called a trident. The net-man was usually the handsomest of the fighters, and the most scantily dressed – he wore just a loincloth. His only armour was a guard on his left arm called a *manica* and a shoulder guard (the *galerus*). His job was to throw his net, with lead weights at the edges, over his opponent and then try to kill him with his trident. This lethal weapon had thick, sharp prongs which could pierce metal. The net-man might finish his opponent off with his dagger (the *pugio*).

This is part of the base of an expensive glass bowl showing a retiarius, with armour and weapons, but no net.

RETIARIUS

ACTION TIME

PLAY THE VICTOR LUDI CARD GAME WITH SOME FRIENDS TO SEE WHO HAS GOT WHAT IT TAKES TO BE A WINNING GLADIATOR.

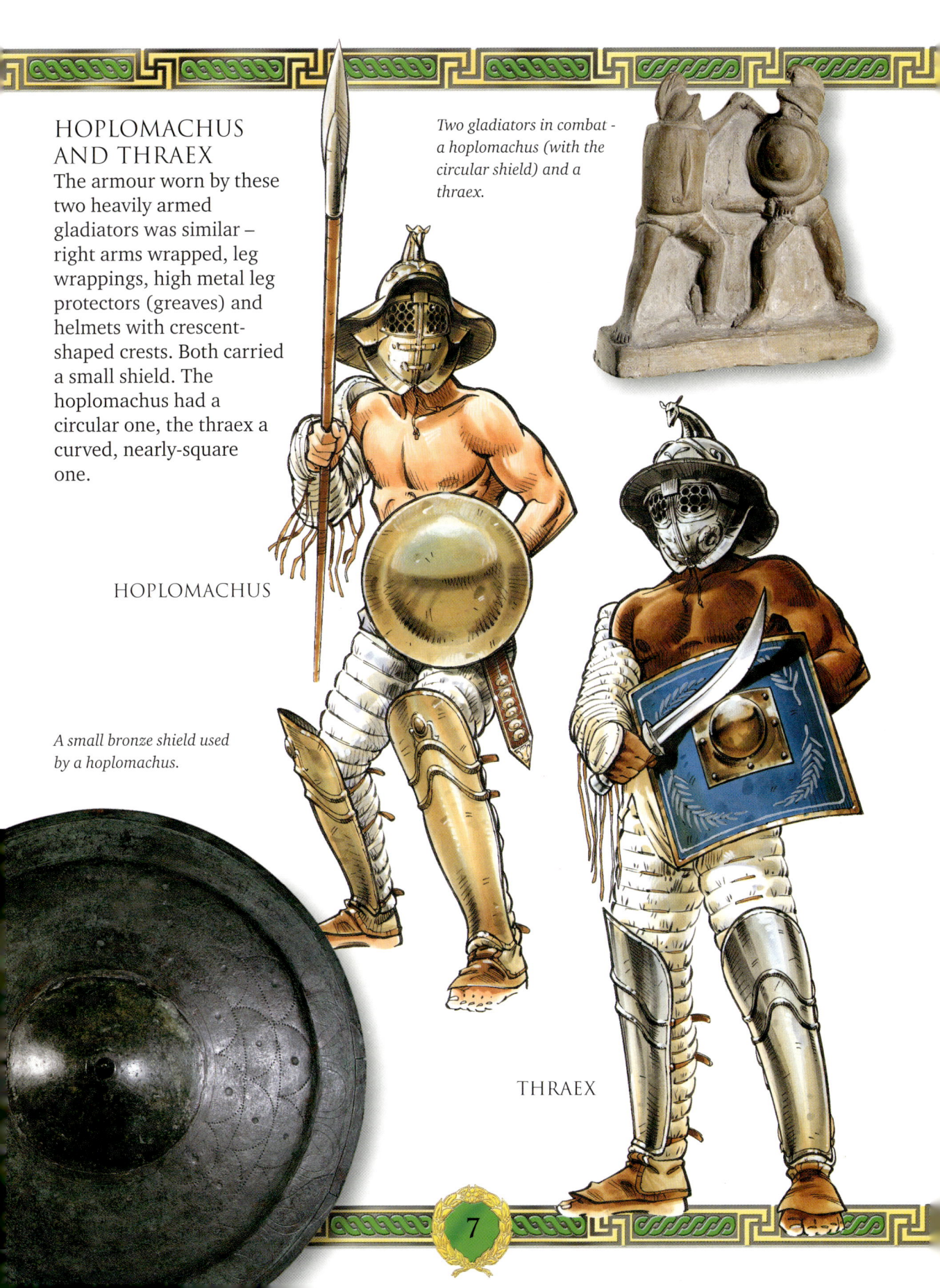

HOPLOMACHUS AND THRAEX

The armour worn by these two heavily armed gladiators was similar – right arms wrapped, leg wrappings, high metal leg protectors (greaves) and helmets with crescent-shaped crests. Both carried a small shield. The hoplomachus had a circular one, the thraex a curved, nearly-square one.

Two gladiators in combat - a hoplomachus (with the circular shield) and a thraex.

HOPLOMACHUS

A small bronze shield used by a hoplomachus.

THRAEX

SECUTOR

The usual opponent of the net-man was called a *secutor* (the pursuer). Unlike his opponent, he was well protected and well armed. His head and neck was covered with a smooth helmet (with only small eye holes) as a protection against the net-man's trident. His right arm had a padded guard and his left leg a metal leg guard (called a greave). He carried the long shield and short stabbing sword of the Roman legionary soldier.

This miniature version of a secutor's helmet shows how well protected the gladiator's head was.

SECUTOR

MURMILLO

This heavily-armed gladiator took his name from a type of fish called *murmuros* because, so Roman writers tell us, he had a fish emblem on his helmet. The helmet was very distinctive with a high crest and wide rim. His other protection was provided by a padded arm-guard on his right arm, thick padded leg coverings with a short metal greave on his left leg, and a rectangular shield. He fought with a short stabbing sword, called the *gladius*, like the swords carried by Roman soldiers. The murmillo fought the hoplomachus or the thraex and then, in the later years of the Roman empire, the retiarius.

MURMILLO

OTHER GLADIATORS' NAMES

EQUES fought on horseback and only against another eques.

CRUPELLARIUS was said to have been so heavily armed that, if he fell down, he could not lift himself up again.

ESSEDARIUS fought from light, fast chariots like those the Romans had seen in the conquest of Britain.

SAGITTARIUS was an archer who may just have fought in the wild animal hunts (see p. 10).

DIMACHAERUS fought with a sword or dagger in each hand.

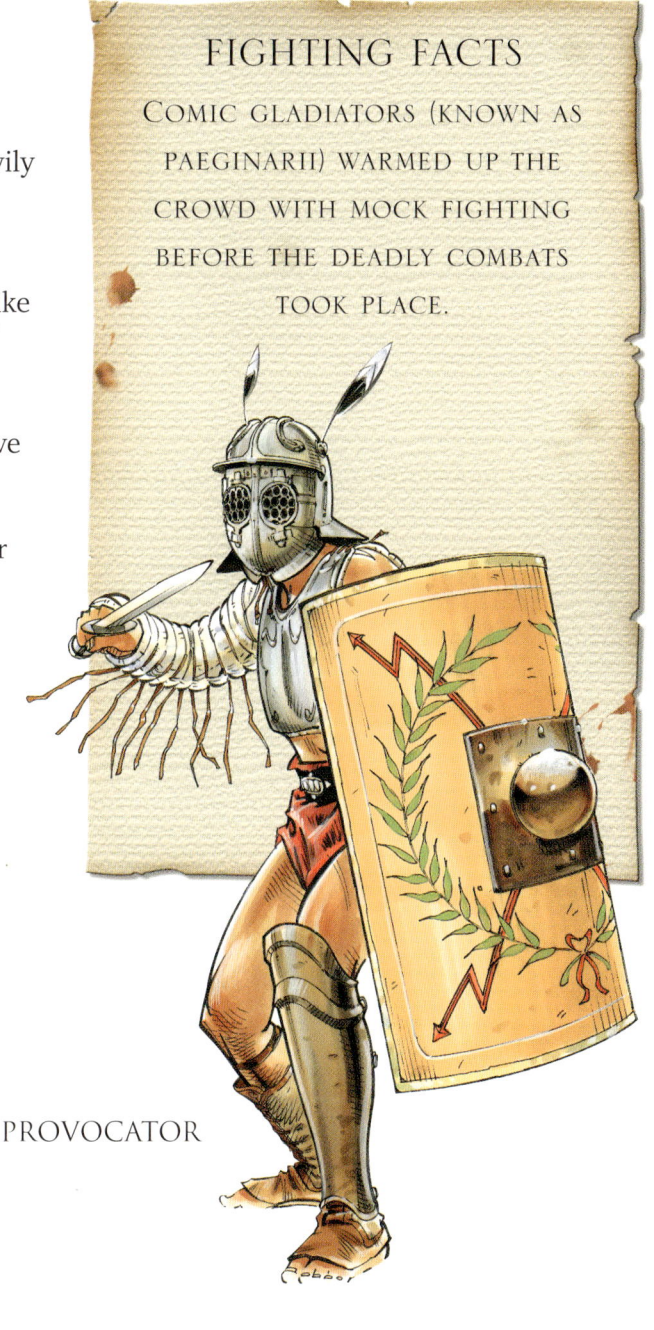

The bronze helmet of a murmillo. Notice the bust of Hercules just below the crest, and how the two halves of the helmet front are fixed together.

FIGHTING FACTS

Comic gladiators (known as paeginarii) warmed up the crowd with mock fighting before the deadly combats took place.

PROVOCATOR

PROVOCATOR

wore a helmet with a visor, had part of his upper body protected by a metal breastplate, had a padded arm-guard and metal leg greaves and carried a sword and a rectangular shield.

ANIMAL HUNTS

The crowds loved the animal hunts (*venationes*) which took place in the amphitheatres in the mornings before the main event when pairs of gladiators fought in the afternoon. There were three events featuring animals – wild animal hunts (by men called *venatores*), animals killing each other, and displays of exotic and performing animals.

This terracotta picture shows a venator (huntsman) about to be attacked by a lioness.

HUNTSMEN
There were special schools to train the men who hunted and killed animals in the amphitheatres – these fighters were called venatores. They fought with spears and wore only tunics and leg wrappings. To help the venatores, there were the bestiarii who looked after the animals and drove them on with whips and burning torches in the arena.

Part of a mosaic from North Africa showing an animal hunt with a bull and a bear fighting.

PROVIDING THE ENTERTAINMENT
At some shows there were only the local beasts, such as bears and bulls, but there were also companies which specialised in the provision of wild animals. They imported them from across the empire and beyond – from North Africa, northern Europe and India, for example. Some emperors used soldiers to capture wild animals for the arena.

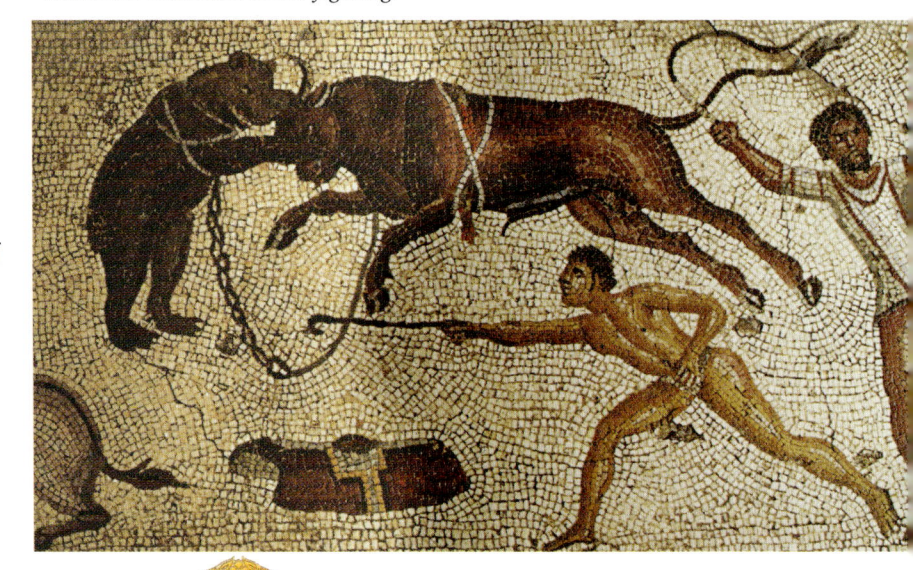

FIGHTING FACTS

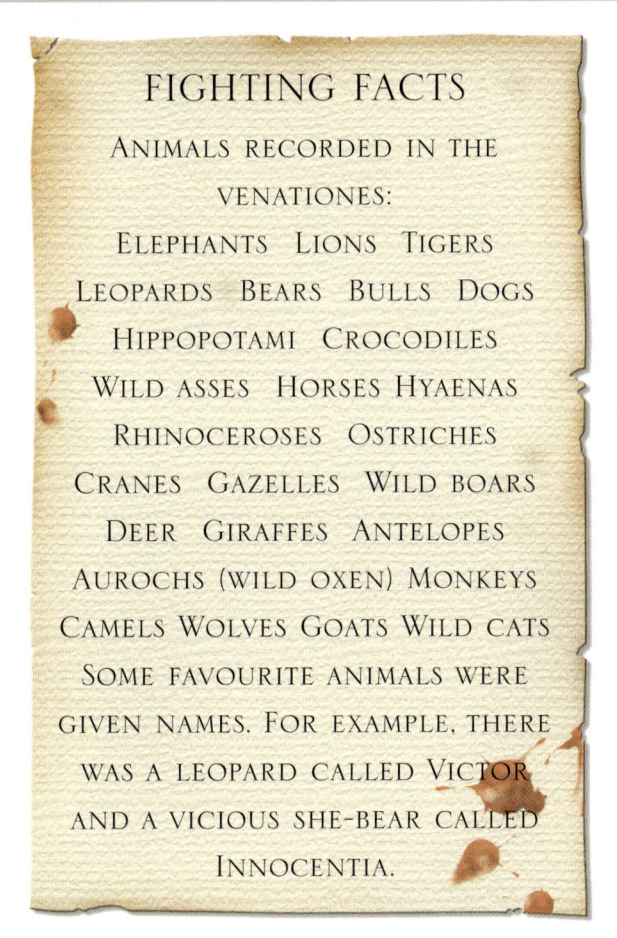

Animals recorded in the venationes:

Elephants Lions Tigers
Leopards Bears Bulls Dogs
Hippopotami Crocodiles
Wild asses Horses Hyaenas
Rhinoceroses Ostriches
Cranes Gazelles Wild boars
Deer Giraffes Antelopes
Aurochs (wild oxen) Monkeys
Camels Wolves Goats Wild cats

Some favourite animals were given names. For example, there was a leopard called Victor and a vicious she-bear called Innocentia.

BRING ON THE ANIMALS

The animals were kept below the surface of the arena just before the shows and brought up in cages through trap doors or up ramps. The Roman crowd loved a spectacle and the organisers sometimes paid for whole landscapes to be created in the arena, with trees, rocks and streams.

This relief carving in marble shows a lion leaping at a hunter (at the top) and then (below) the lion attacking him. The inscription says, 'He was taken away for burial.'

PUBLIC EXECUTIONS

The Roman authorities also used wild animals to perform particularly horrific executions on criminals or slaves who were condemned to be punished by their owners. These unfortunate people might be tied to stakes or covered with animal skins to be hunted and torn to pieces by wild animals. Christians and Jews, who refused to accept the Roman gods, were often condemned to death in the arena.

Victims for execution were sometimes tied to trolleys and pushed towards wild animals.

WOMEN GLADIATORS

There were women who fought as gladiators, although they were not very well thought of by the Roman spectators. We know from reading accounts by some Roman writers that there were women who fought as armed gladiators and as fighters on chariots. Some high-born women even chose to fight like the male noblemen (see page 2 or 3). Writers also tell us that they were rather a 'novelty act'. The emperor Septimius Severus banned female gladiators in AD 200.

FIGHTING WOMEN

This carving shows two female gladiators, each dressed as a murmillo gladiator. The inscription tells us that their stage names were Amazon and Achillia (named after the Greek hero, Achilles) and that they were given their freedom. The carving comes from Halicarnassus, now Bodrum in Turkey.

FIGHTING FACTS

A SPEARHEAD WITH WHICH A GLADIATOR HAD BEEN KILLED WAS THOUGHT TO BE A GOOD OMEN AT A BRIDE'S WEDDING!

FANATICAL FANS

Roman gladiators had their fan clubs, just like footballers today. There were two sorts of fanatical fans. Fans who followed the gladiators who carried a large shield were called *scutarii*. Those who preferred the small shield were the *parmularii*. Successful gladiators attracted women followers – someone wrote on a wall in Pompeii that the gladiator Celado was a 'heart throb'. Scratched on a piece of pottery found in Leicester were the words 'Verecunda the dancer, Lucius the gladiator'. It had a hole pierced in it so it was probably a love token.

A small glass container for perfume, in the shape of a secutor's helmet.

Drawn on a wall in Pompeii, a murmillo (left) defeats a thraex called Raecius Felix.

AT THE COLOSSEUM

The Colosseum was the largest of all Roman amphitheatres. It is 188 by 156 metres and, according to Roman records, could hold 45,000 spectators who poured in to see the games through 80 entrances. It was begun by the emperor Vespasian and completed in AD 80.

WATCHING THE GAMES
Officials and high-ranking spectators occupied the first two tiers, nearest the action. Then came a tier for the middle classes and the highest tier for lower classes, slaves, women and children. To shade the spectators from the burning sun, hundreds of workers winched up a huge awning to cover the whole building.

The Colosseum has now lost the wooden floor, covered with sand, which covered the underground passages and rooms. Wild animals were kept in the rooms below the arena.

OPENING CEREMONY
On the morning of the games there were the animal hunts followed at midday by the executions of criminals. The formal opening of the games in the afternoon was always spectacular. The official who paid for the games (the *editor*) led a solemn procession of gladiators, trainers, referees, condemned criminals and the armour and weapon carriers.

PREPARING FOR THE GAMES
Painted advertisements on walls let the public know who was going to fight and when. A few days before the start of the games, the gladiators were shown off to the crowds in the town's square. The evening before the show a public banquet was held for the performers.

Left: the outside surviving wall of the Colosseum. For centuries after the Roman period it was robbed of its stone for other buildings in Rome.

FIGHTING FACTS
The Romans loved displays on water, called *NAUMACHIA*. Famous naval battles were re-fought in flooded amphitheatres or on lakes.

The first record of *NAUMACHIA* was of Julius Caesar constructing a lake in Rome in 46 BC to celebrate a triumph. In AD 52 the emperor Claudius put on a sea battle with a hundred ships and 19,000 convicted criminals dressed as sailors.

ACTION TIME
You can stage your own games with the press-out gladiator figures in the kit. Open out the survival kit and stand it up to create the backdrop for your arena. Decide the fate of your fighters – live or die? – with the pull-tab.

This mosaic from North Africa shows a group of musicians playing in an amphitheatre.

Left: a model of an organ, similar to the one shown in the mosaic, powered by water and compressed air.

Below: a trumpet and a pair of cymbals.

THE SHOW BEGINS

The opening events were exciting and amusing – there were the warm-up gladiators clowning, men on stilts provoking wild animals and displays by horse riders, acrobats and jugglers. After all that the serious fighting started. Musicians were on hand for the opening ceremony and the gladiatorial performances. There were trumpets and horns, woodwind instruments called tibiae, and organs.

Any gladiator who fought well might be given his freedom. This inscribed plaque records the release given to a gladiator called Moderatus by his owner Lucceius on 5 October AD 88.

WINNER OR LOSER?

The sponsor of the games, who might have been the emperor, sat in a special area (like the directors' box at a football match). It was up to him to spare a defeated fighter, grant his freedom, or order his death.

© 2004 The Trustees of The British Museum

First published in 2004 by British Museum Press, a division of The British Museum Company Ltd, 46 Bloomsbury Street, London WC1B 3QQ

ISBN 0 7141 3104 0
A catalogue record for this title is available from the British Library

Designed and typeset by HERRING BONE DESIGN.
Printed and bound in China.

Gladiator colour illustrations by Chris West/Black Hat. Photographs © The Trustees of the British Museum unless otherwise stated. Colchester Museums p. 3. Roger Wood/Corbis p. 2 bottom; p. 10 bottom, p. 11 bottom; p. 16 top left. Mike Corbishley p. 14; p. 15. Museo Archeologico Nazionale di Napoli p. 13 bottom. Museum of London p. 2 top.

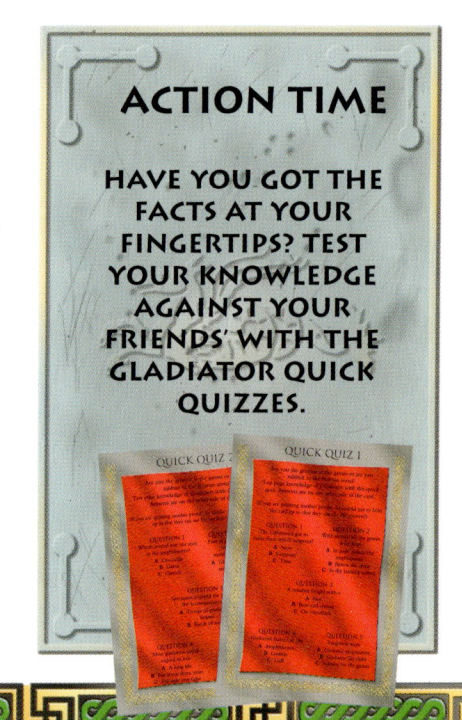

ACTION TIME

HAVE YOU GOT THE FACTS AT YOUR FINGERTIPS? TEST YOUR KNOWLEDGE AGAINST YOUR FRIENDS' WITH THE GLADIATOR QUICK QUIZZES.